The Global Labour Movement: An Introduction

A short guide to the Global Union Federations, the ITUC, and other international bodies

Edited by

Edd Mustill

Introduced by

Eric Lee

CONTENTS

INTRODUCTION

Eric Lee, founding editor, LabourStart

There are two things I never expect to hear when people talk to me about this book.

The first is, "What? Another book on the global labour movement?"

And second is, "*Fifty Shades of Red* would have been a better title."

Of course there have been other books about the global labour movement. I have several of them on my shelf. I have seen some in libraries.

But I have not seen a book like this one, and certainly not in the hands of the people who actually make up that movement.

We need an introductory book about the global labour movement for the same reason that we need the movement itself.

We need a book like this because our movement is facing new challenges in an increasingly globalised world and our members need to understand those challenges.

I'll be honest: it pains me when I hear a trade unionist, and sometimes even a trade union leader, say that what we need today are unions which, like multinational corporations, don't recognise borders, or that we need to create a new model of trade unionism which can mobilize workers around the world in pursuit of our common interests.

Of course we need that – but I always want to respond by saying that (a) we've known this for more than 150 years and that's what the phrase "workers of all countries unite" was all about and (b) there already is a global labour movement.

We don't need to invent one, we just need to make this one stronger and more effective.

Making the global labour movement stronger is a no-brainer. Obviously we need much more powerful institutions at global level to take on corporations as powerful as, say, Wal-Mart. But to convince everyone in our unions that strong global labour institutions are essential, people have got to know what already exists.

Because the fact is that we have global union federations that have been doing amazing work for a century or more – even if most members of their affiliated unions have never heard of them.

And we've got a federation of all the world's leading national trade union centres which, incredibly, is not a household name.

Everyone has heard of Amnesty International, which does

amazing work (more on that in a moment), and has around 3 million supporters.

But for every member of Amnesty, there are nearly 60 members of the trade unions organised into the International Trade Union Confederation (ITUC).

Never heard of the ITUC? With 175 million members? That's why we wrote this book.

But before we dive in to all that, I want to say a few words about the past, present and future of the global labour movement.

One could argue that the global labour movement emerged in 1847 when Marx and Engels famously ended the Communist Manifesto with these sentences:

"The proletarians have nothing to lose but their chains. They have a world to win. Workers of the world, unite!"

Of course they were not the first to suggest such a thing and they would have acknowledged that the modern labour movement had it origins in many earlier struggles.

But from 1847 until today, we've had a global labour movement in different forms.

The formation of the International Working Men's Association (known as the "First International") back in 1864 marked a highlight of course, but it disappeared within a few years.

What is extraordinary is not the disappearance of something like the "First International" – students of these things can point to many similar institutions that have arisen and disappeared over the last century and a half – but the endurance of some of what are now known as global union federations.

The International Metalworkers Federation, which last year merged with two other federations to become IndustriALL, was founded in 1893. The International Transport Workers Federation was founded three years later.

The IMF and the ITF have been at it for nearly 120 years. Some of the other global union federations are nearly as old.

The ITUC traces its origins back to the First International, and in 2014 will commemorate the 150th anniversary of the founding of the International Working Men's Association at its own world congress to be held in Berlin.

Over the course of those many decades, names have changed, and ideas have changed, and yet trade unions endure and with them their own particular global institutions.

It's very common to say that we need something now, more than ever. Politicians are fond of that expression. But when it comes to the global unions, it really is true.

Back in 1896, when transport workers came up with the idea of a global federation, could they have imagined what the transport business would look like in the 21st century?

The ITF was founded before the Wright Brothers had succeeded in the invention of heavier-than-air flight. Most transportation networks at that time – except for ocean-crossing steamships – were local or national.

You might have made the case if you were a metal worker back in 1893 that you didn't really see the point of your union affililating to, and paying dues to, some new-fangled "International Metalworkers' Federation". After all, your employers were local or national firms.

But today, if you're a worker at a Japanese-owned auto factory in Mississippi, facing a company that refuses to recognise your union (but is happy to deal with unions back home), you probably get the importance of solidarity in a way your great-great-grandfather might not have. Or you should get it, anyway.

Of course, it's not that simple. Labour historians will be quick to point out that the idea of global working-class solidarity was in fact quite popular in the 1890s. There are many extraordinary stories about workers in one country rallying to support their comrades in others – long before anyone ever heard about "globalisation."

One of the strange things about our time is that we as a movement have forgotten much of this at precisely the moment when we need to be more internationalist than ever before.

And this book has been produced to help us do that. To remind us as a movement of who we are, of our traditions and our strength.

In the pages that follow, we've put together essential information on each of the global union federations. You'll learn who they represent, how they're organised, how to get in touch with them and so on.

But you'll also learn where they come from – and what they do today.

Of course we have information about the International Trade Union Confederation, but we also explore some of the institutions of the global labour movement that you may never have heard of, such as the Council of Global Unions and the Trade Union Advisory Committe to the OECD.

We asked for some of our friends in the global unions to help us explore other aspects of our movement.

In the section on the global union federations, you'll find a couple of short interviews with union leaders who explain how they've benefited from their union's involvement with a global union.

And we've got a short essay by Owen Tudor of Britain's Trades Union Congress, giving us a picture of how one national trade union centre engages in global solidarity work.

The global labour movement is more than just trade unions – we can include in our family groups like Amnesty International, whose trade union coordinator Shane Enright has given us a short introduction to their work.

Daniel Blackburn of the International Centre for Trade Union Rights writes about his organisation's work promoting union rights around the world.

Dave Spooner has contributed a short piece about the Global Labour Institute – a relatively new addition to the global labour movement's family.

So let me conclude by thanking all those who contributed to this book, including those not named here, and in particular Edd Mustill for doing a fantastic job of pulling it all together.

THE GLOBAL UNION FEDERATIONS

THE BUILDING AND WOODWORKERS INTERNATIONAL

WWW.BWINT.ORG

The global union for workers in the building, wood, and forestry industries.

*The BWI represents **12** million workers across **350** unions in **135** countries.*

PRESIDENT
Klaus Wiesehügel

GENERAL SECRETARY
Albert Emilio Yuson

BWI
54 route des Acacias
CH-1227 Carouge GE
Switzerland

Tel.: + 41 22 827 37 77
Fax: + 41 22 827 37 70
Email: info@bwint.org

HISTORY

The Building and Woodworkers International (BWI) was founded in 2005, through a merger of the International Federation of Building and Wood Workers (IFBWW), and the World Federation of Building and Woodworkers (WFBW). The IFBWW had a membership of 10.5 million, while the WFBW was a smaller federation of 1.5 million, which had its genesis in the Christian union movement.

STRUCTURE

The BWI's World Congress meets every four years. It elects a President, Deputy-President, and General Secretary, as well as a World Council. The World Council, which meets twice a year, in turn appoints regional representatives to sit on the World Board, which is responsible for administration and implementing policy. The World Council also establishes an International Women's Committee. There are also Regional Committees for Africa, Latin America and the Caribbean, Asia and the Pacific, Europe, and North America.

CAMPAIGNING

Construction is one of the world's most dangerous industries, with the International Labour Organisation estimating that at least 60,000 deaths occur on sites annually – or one every ten minutes. Because of this, much BWI campaigning is around health and safety. Many of the world's high profile sporting projects cause death and injury on construction sites. In the run up to the Euro 2012 football championships in Poland and Ukraine, the BWI did much to highlight the terrible working conditions of those building the stadiums. They are currently running a Campaign for Decent Work in Brazil in the run up to the Fifa World Cup there in 2014.

In India, the BWI has campaigned against the use of child labour in the brick kiln industry. It has provided financial and technical support for unions to set up schools, which have successfully pulled over 10,000 children out of work and into education, while at the same time teaching them about union rights.

As a global union, the BWI pushes transnational companies to sign up to International Framework Agreements based on the core conventions of the ILO. These agreements allow local unions to start to organise more easily and get recognised. They have successfully negotiated agreements with giants like Skanska and IKEA.

EDUCATION INTERNATIONAL

WWW.EI-IE.ORG

The global union for employees in the education sector.

*EI represents **30** million workers across **400** unions in **170** countries.*

PRESIDENT
Susan Hopgood

GENERAL SECRETARY
Fred van Leeuwen

5 boulevard du Roi Albert II
B-1210 Brussels
Belgium

Tel: +32-2 224 06 11
Fax: -32-2 224 06 06
Email: headoffice@ei-ie.org

HISTORY

EI can trace its lineage back at least to 1912, when the first attempt to bring teachers organisations together took place in Belgium, but it wasn't until 1926 that the International Trade Secretariat for teachers was founded. (International Trade Secretariat was the old name for Global Union Federation.)

Like the rest of the international movement, teachers' organisations were split by the Cold War, with Communist-supporting unions forming the World Federation of Teachers' Unions (FISE, from its French name). However, teachers were fractured even more because of the existence of two separate federations in the non-Communist world: The World Confederation of Organisations of the Teaching Profession (WCOTP) and the International Federation of Free Teachers' Unions (IFFTU).

The IFFTU was more staunchly anti-Communist, thanks largely to the influence of the American Federation of Labor and the American Federation of Teachers. While the ideological lines were sharply drawn in developed countries, many unions in other parts of the world affiliated to both secretariats, simply in order to receive as much international assistance as they could. As a result, WCOTP included organisations that were affiliated to the Communist FISE, and others affiliated to the staunchly anti-Communist IFFTU.

The WCOTP tended to attract organisations that saw themselves more as professional associations, whereas the IFFTU's affiliates tended to identify more strongly as labour unions. IFFTU remained much the smaller of the two groups until the 1960s, when teachers' unions began to engage in more traditional union activities, for example the first major American teachers' strike in 1967. The idea that teachers' organisations should be engaged in collective bargaining and fighting on workplace issues began to take hold. While EI maintains a commitment to professionalism in the sense that it argues for teachers to be fully trained and qualified, it has very much adopted the methods of unionism.

WCOTP and IFFTU only merged at a conference in Stockholm in 1993, the culmination of years of negotiations going back into the mid-1980s. The 1993 Congress affirmed the right of education for all. EI also committed itself to championing education in a broader sense, including education for democracy, human rights, and respect for diversity. Founding president Albert Shanker made the point that an excellent education system cannot work in isolation from wider society. If children going to schools are affected by poverty, violence, and discrimination in their communities, a school system can only achieve so much. So EI committed itself to fighting these wider social ills.

In 2007, EI completed its merger with the World Confederation of Teachers, which had come from the Christian Democratic tradition. South African teacher Thulas Nxesi led EI for the next four years, before becoming a minister in the ANC government.

STRUCTURE

The World Congress of EI meets every four years, with delegates present from all affiliates. The Congress agrees a four year programme of policy and financial decisions. The last Congress in 2011 considered motions on topics as diverse as climate change, union rights in South Korea, and organising student teachers.

Congress elects an Executive Board which meets at least once a year to oversee EI's activities. The board is made up of offices, two representatives from each global region, and a number of open seats.

EI has a solidarity fund to which each affiliate is asked to contribute 0.7% of their income. This is used to assist affiliates facing particularly harsh conditions, such as those operating in war zones or the aftermath of natural disasters such as the Indian Ocean tsunami of 2004.

CAMPAIGNING

As an organisation of teachers' unions, the nature of a lot of EI's campaigning is around social as well as workplace issues, in the sense that it is seeking to influence or fight against the education policies of governments. EI holds that quality education is a human right to which all are entitled, and that education should be provided by the public sector. To this end, EI will launch a global campaign, Standing Up for Quality Education, in October 2013.

EI takes the UNESCO-ILO Recommendation on the Status of Teachers of 1966 as a starting point for teachers' rights. This confirms the status of teachers as qualified professionals, and EI opposes any de-skilling of the teaching profession. Their Quality Educators for All project, in partnership with the Dutch affiliate of Oxfam, aims to do this by working with governments and institutions around the world to improve the quality of teacher training.

EI also backs professional status for support staff, and have welcomed a campaign launched by one of their affiliates, the New Zealand Educational Institute, to that end. Its policy, as adopted at the last World Congress, states: "EI affirms that support staff should have the same status, rights and conditions as other education employees with comparable academic and technical qualifications and experience."

Many parts of the world are far from safe places for teacher unionists. Since 2011, EI has been involved in a long running prominent campaign for the release of jailed leaders of its Bahraini affiliate, the Bahrain Teachers' Association. Jalila al-Salman and Mahdi abu Deeb were both imprisoned for their role in the peaceful democratic uprising in Bahrain, during which they led a teachers strike and appealed for the support of parents and students.

Colombia remains a dangerous place for teacher trade unionists. Over one thousand have been killed in the country since 1995. EI have previously used their solidarity fund to help threatened teachers safely escape the country.

INDUSTRIALL

WWW.INDUSTRIALL-UNION.ORG

The global union for workers in mining, energy, and manufacturing.

IndustiALL represents 50 million workers in 140 countries.

PRESIDENT
Berthold Huber

GENERAL SECRETARY
Jyrki Raina

54 bis, route des Acacias, Case
Postale 1516
1227 Geneva
Switzerland

Tel: + 41 22 308 5050
Telefax: + 41 22 308 5055
Email: info@industriall-
union.org

HISTORY

IndustriALL is the youngest of the global union federations. It was founded on 19th June 2012 through the merger of the International Metalworkers Federation (IMF), the International Federation of Chemical, Energy, Mine and General Workers' Unions (ICEM), and the International Textile, Garment, and Leather Workers' Federation (ITGLWF).

As IndustriALL represents the industrial sectors of the economy where unions first emerged, it is perhaps not surprising that its heritage stretches back a long way. One of the union's predecessors, the Miners' International Federation, was founded in Belgium in 1890, calling for an eight hour day, vast improvement in health and safety, and the abolition of child labour in the mines.

The International Metalworkers' Federation was founded in Zurich in 1893, during a Congress of socialist parties from around Europe. Very quickly, it was able to facilitate collections and donations from metalworkers across the continents to support their striking comrades. German unions supported both British and Danish workers during their long lock-outs in 1897.

Also in 1893, international craft-oriented organisations were formed for shoe-makers, leatherworkers, and others in the clothing industries. These were mainly concerned with providing information on wages and conditions in other countries and supporting migrant workers travelling between countries in Europe in search of work.

Factory workers founded their own organisation in Stuttgart in 1907, at the time of the International Socialist Congress there. Like many of the early secretariats, their development was cut short with the outbreak of the First World War, but they re-emerged as the Federation of General Factory Workers, under the leadership of German unionist August Brey, in 1920. In 1929, they set up an international strike fund for affiliate members.

The rise of European fascism and the Second World War hit manufacturing unions hard. The Factory Workers' Amsterdam office was closed just six days after the Nazi invasion of the Netherlands in 1940, and their then general secretary Klaas de Jonge was imprisoned in a concentration camp for the duration of the war. Bruno Buozzi, President of the Italian metalworkers union and active in the IMF, was one of countless trade unionists killed while operating underground during the war.

Both the miners and factory workers' were able to rebuild after the Second World War. The factory workers soon merged with international secretariats of glass and ceramics unions, while the miners expanded to cover the new nuclear power industry. The IMF also grew in the late 1940s, picking up strong unions like Force Ouvriere in France and Federazione Italiana Metalmeccanici in Italy. In 1948, the new amalgamated union for metalworkers in West Germany, IG Metall, joined, followed in the next year by the powerful United Auto Workers (UAW) and United Steelworkers (USW) in America.

Throughout the 1950s, against the backdrop of the post-war economic upswing, metalworkers unions across Europe pushed for and won shorter working weeks. They were supported by the IMF's Economic and Social Department, which also helped the USW obtain a national agreement by using its global knowledge to expel the bosses' myths that wages in America were "too high."

The post-war period also saw the industrial unions expand out from their traditional European and North American base for the first time. In 1964, the IMF brought together fractured Japanese manufacturing unions in a national council, as it had done for the British engineering unions half a century earlier, helping to speed up the process of achieve unity in the workplace. National councils soon followed in Malaysia, the Philippines, and Taiwan.

In Africa the National Union of Mineworkers (NUM) and the National Union of Metalworkers of South Africa (NUMSA) and in Latin America the Confederação Nacional dos Metalúrgicos (CNM-CUT – Brazil), Confederacão Nacional dos Ramos Quimicos (CNQ/CUT – Brazil), Confederación Nacional de Trabajadores Metalúrgicos (CONSTRAMET – Chile) and the Unión Nacional de Trabajadores del Metal y Ramas Afines (UNTMRA – Uruguay) played a crucial role in the foundation of IMF and ICEM in their respective regions of the world.

The other industrial secretariats also expanded. Textile and shoe workers' organisations merged in 1970 to form the ITGLWF. In the 1970s the Factory Workers, now renamed as the International Federation of Chemical and General Workers Unions (ICF), picked up a number of member unions who fell away from the International Federation of Petroleum and Chemical Workers. In 1995, the chemical workers and miners finally merged to form the ICEM.

Meanwhile, the IMF grew again in the late '80s and early '90s, as a result of the collapse of Stalinism. The IMF was quick to make contact with metalworkers unions in eastern Europe as they emerged out of the shadow of state control.

The industrial global unions managed to survive the decimation of jobs in the manufacturing sector in Europe and North America that has occurred over the last few decades, and expand into others parts of the world, paving the way for the merger in 2012.

STRUCTURE

The IndustriALL founding congress in 2012 elected the organisation's president and general secretary, and their deputies. Also elected was a 60-strong executive committee, with members representing six global regions. This will be reduced in size to 40 at the next Congress in 2016.

Future Congresses will take place at least every four years. At least 30% of each union's delegation to Congress must be made up of women where possible.

IndustriALL maintains regional offices in Johannesburg,

New Delhi, Singapore, Moscow, and Montevideo.

The union has sectoral as well as regional structures. Unions are eligible for affiliation of they represent manual or non-manual workers in a number of industries, including aerospace, electronics, mining, chemicals, shipbuilding, and textiles. Affiliates must be democratic and free from the influence of governments and employers.

CAMPAIGNING

In its founding action plan, IndustriALL says it will "create a global organization capable of challenging the power of multinational companies (MNCs) and negotiating with them on a global level."

One of IndustriALL's priorities is the establishment of Global Framework Agreements (GFAs) across the supply chain of multinational companies. GFAs have been signed with companies including auto company Ford, cement giant Lafarge (together with the BWI), Siemens, and Brazilian energy company Petrobras. GFAs commit companies to recognising workers' rights to freedom of association, and often also include other core principles around, for example, rates of pay, or the recognition of ILO guidelines.

IndustriALL has supported its affiliates acting in solidarity with one another. In March 2013, members of the South African union CEPPWAWU struck for one and a half days at Unilever, in solidarity with Dutch workers whose jobs were being outsourced by the company to Sodexo, with a resulting loss of pension benefits. IndustriALL has worked with the International Union of Foodworkers to set up a strong global network of unions in the company, the founding meeting of which pledged itself to campaign for "sustainable workplaces, sustainable employment and guarantees of rights for current and future Unilever workers."

To strengthen workers' bargaining positions, IndustriALL has brought together several of its Zimbabwean affiliates with a view to helping them towards a merger and strengthening their financial position in one of the world's most dire economies.

The union has taken the lead in securing compensation for the families of victims of garment factory fires in Bangladesh, negotiating with well-known brands like New Look who are the at the end of the industry's supply chain and bear social responsibility for conditions in the factories. In early 2013, IndustriALL negotiated a tripartite fire safety agreement with employers' associations and the Bangladesh government, as part of the long process of stamping out the fires in the garment industry.

Every February, IndustriALL organises days of action in support of Mexican workers, to commemorate and fight for justice for the 65 miners who died at Pasta de Conchos on 19th February 2006. The actions also coalesce around other demands, including the rights of workers to hold union elections free from the intimidation of management and yellow unions.

IndustriALL's "Stop Precarious Work" campaign highlights the global trend towards the use of agency labour and other forms of casual work. As much as 60% of Mexico's electronics industry is run on casual labour, and 30% of Nokia's

Chinese workforce, with similar figures around the world. IndustriALL affiliates like the Indian National Mineworkers Federation (INMF) have in recent years made a big push to organise precarious workers and bring them in to the union fold. The INMF has recruited some 66,869 such workers in the last decade. In January 2013, IndustriALL's Indonesian affiliates won a huge victory, forcing the government to change the status of 16-20 million workers from outsourced to permanent employees.

Recognising that "there are no jobs on a dead planet," IndustriALL is at the forefront of fighting for sustainable manufacturing industries. Many industrial workers do jobs that are dangerous both to themselves and the environment. The long running campaign against the atrocious conditions in the ship-breaking industry, where huge ships are often broken up on the coast of the Indian subcontinent with little regard for safety or pollution, is an example of this. IndustriALL estimates that up to 120,000 workers in South Asia are exposed to hazardous materials during shipbreaking, without any health and safety training. The union, with the help of the Dutch national trade union centre FNV, has organised thousands of shipbreaking workers in India in the last decade.

INTERNATIONAL FEDERATION OF ACTORS

WWW.FIA-ACTORS.COM

The global union for actors and performers.

PRESIDENT
Ferne Downey

GENERAL SECRETARY
Dominick Luquer

International Federation of Actors
(FIA)
40, rue Joseph II b/04
1000 Brussels
Belgium

Tel: +32 (0)2 235 08 74
Fax: +32 (0)2 235 08 70

History

The International Federation of Actors (FIA) has its origins in a meeting called by the French actors' union Syndicat National des Acteurs Français in Paris in 1951. Under the leadership of Jean Darcante, the French union brought together actors unions from across Europe. The FIA's founding congress took place the following year in London, and soon it spread beyond Europe when the Mexican Asociacion Nacional de Actores joined.

The FIA attracted affiliates from both sides of the iron curtain at a time when the international labour movement was deeply divided; the Cuban and Polish unions joined in the mid 1950s, and in the late 1960s actors unions from both the United States and the Soviet Union affiliated.

The experimental introduction of television to Europe in the early 1950s gave the FIA its first dispute. It instructed its members, in partnership with the musicians' and variety artists' organisations, not to work on TV shows destined for overseas broadcast until an international agreement on fees was reached. This was successfully achieved in 1956, one of the earliest examples of international collective bargaining.

The growth of TV led to the FIA having to deal with some unique problems. For example, actors didn't want reruns of their shows being used during strikes in the industry in other countries, which effectively turned them into strike-breakers through no fault of their own. The Europe-wide agreement negotiated by the FIA had a provision to deal with this.

STRUCTURE

The FIA Congress meets every four years, and elects an Executive Committee which meets annually. In between meetings of the Executive Committee, the Presidum, made up of the President and six Vice-Presidents, may meet to make decisions on matters of urgency.

Regions of the FIA hold their own meetings and can elect their own officers. As well as national unions, local organisations of actors may affiliate at the discretion of the Executive Committee.

FIA works with the International Federation of Musicians, and the Media, Entertainment, and Arts section of UNI Global Union, in an umbrella organisation called the International Arts and Entertainment Alliance.

CAMPAIGNING

The FIA's most high profile campaign in recent years has been to campaign for union contracts during the filming of the *Hobbit* trilogy in New Zealand. They drew attention to the fact that, while most international stars of the films were covered by union contracts, many actors in the New Zealand industry were not. The FIA rallied unions internationally to call for their members not to work on the film unless the producers agreed to union contracts.

In 2009-10, the European region of the FIA ran an education project of seminars and conferences aiming to challenge stereotypical portrayals of gender in film, TV, and theatre.

The FIA has also generated solidarity for its affiliates around facing various problems. It has supported dubbing artists in Hungary, who are paid very low rates in a country where all foreign TV is dubbed, and campaigned for the release from prison of Burmese actor U Muang Thura.

INTERNATIONAL FEDERATION OF JOURNALISTS

WWW.IFJ.ORG

The global union for journalists.

*IFJ represents **600,000** members in **174** unions across **120** countries.*

PRESIDENT
Jim Boumelha

GENERAL SECRETARY
Elisabeth Costa

IPC-Residence Palace, Bloc C
Rue de la Loi 155
B-1040 Brussels
Belgium

Tel: 32-2-235 22 00
Fax: 32-2-235 22 19
E-Mail: ifj@ifj.org

HISTORY

The International Federation of Journalists (IFJ) was founded in 1926. After the Second World War, along with much of the rest of the union movement, journalists' unions were divided between the East and West, with the Soviet-influenced International Organisation of Journalists operating out of Prague until the end of the Cold War.

STRUCTURE

Congress takes place every three years. Extraordinary Congresses can be called by a two-thirds majority of the Executive Committee, or a simple majority of affiliated organisations. The Executive Committee, elected by Congress, consists of the Federation's officers and 16 other members. No more than one delegate from any one country can be elected to the EC in this way. It meets twice a year.

Journalists' unions which are committed to press freedom are eligible to affiliate. Unions that are organised across the media industry can affiliate, but only the section of their membership who are actually journalists makes up their affiliated membership for the purposes of votes at Congress. Other, non-union, journalists organisations which are committed to press freedom are eligible to be admitted as associate members.

CAMPAIGNING

The IFJ exists both to safeguard and extend the freedom of journalists, and the freedom of the press more generally. The Federation campaigns for the release of journalists jailed for criticising authoritarian governments around the world. It is currently rallying support for its two affiliates in Ukraine, the Independent Media Trade Union and the National Union of Journalists of Ukraine, to fight against the introduction of criminal liability for defamation, a disproportionate measure that would intimidate journalists out of making accusations against the rich and powerful.

The IFJ stands for freedom of the press universally. They have campaigned for the release of Palestinian journalists in Israeli prisons, as well as the lifting of restrictions on journalists in Hamas-controlled Gaza. The Federation also calls out hypocrisy; in 2009, it refused to participate in UNESCO's World Press Freedom Day celebrations in Qatar, because that country did not allow journalists their own union.

INTERNATIONAL FEDERATION OF MUSICIANS

WWW.FIM-MUSICIANS.ORG

The global union for musicians.

PRESIDENT
John Smith

GENERAL SECRETARY
Benoit Machuel

21 bis rue Victor Massé
F-75009 Paris
France

Tel: +33 (0) 145 263 123
Fax: +33 (0) 176 701 418
Email: office@fim-
musicians.org

International Transport Workers Federation

WWW.ITFGLOBAL.ORG

The global union workers in the seafaring, docks, civil aviation, rail transport, and road transport industries.

*IFJ represents **4.5 million** workers in **700** unions across **150** countries.*

PRESIDENT
Paddy Crumlin

GENERAL SECRETARY
David Cockcroft

ITF House
49-60 Borough Road
London SE1 1DR
United Kingdom

Tel: +44 20 7403 2733
Email: mail@itf.org.uk

History

The International Transport Workers Federation (ITF) was founded in London in 1896 as the International Federation of Ship, Dock, and River Workers. The nature of international trade through shipping meant that transport workers were perhaps the first to realise the importance of global solidarity in industrial disputes, and the founding of the Federation itself was a response to a call for help from striking dockers in Rotterdam. Just a few short years earlier the great dock strike of 1889 had shaken English ports, and its leaders Tom Mann and Ben Tillett were among the early leaders of the International Federation. Mann himself was arrested during the Hamburg dock strike of 1896-7 and deported back to England.

The ITF grew steadily in a period of increasing militancy among transport workers, before the outbreak of the First World War cut this short. Nevertheless, the organisation managed to survive and return to action after the armistice. After the Russian Revolution, they helped organise boycotts of munitions going to the White armies in Russia, and to Admiral Horthy's proto-fascist regime in Hungary. Nevertheless, the ITF was damaged by the foundation of the "Red International of Labour Unions," which attracted some

Communist-supporting transport workers to its ranks.

In the 1920s, the ITF began to agitate against the racist atti-
tudes of some of its own members and unions. Secretary Edo
Fimmen argued for workers around the world to see their
struggle as one, and that unions in the West would lose any
gains they made "unless they take energetic steps to improve
the standard of living in the Eastern countries." In 1923-24,
rail unions from Palestine, Argentina, India, and Indonesia
all affiliated to the ITF.

As fascism spread in Europe, the ITF helped distribute "ille-
gal" union material to unions in Germany, as well as providing material aid to the Spanish Republic during the Civil War
there. As powerful and often militant workforces, transport
workers were often the first to be repressed, persecuted, and
killed by fascists. Hermann Jochade, who had led the ITF
between 1904-16, was killed in a Nazi concentration camp in
1939.

After the war, the ITF expanded into the global South, with
unions across Africa affiliating. A first Latin American Transport Workers Conference took place in 1949, followed by an
Asian Transport Workers Conference was held in 1955. In the
1960s, ITF membership across Africa and Latin America
grew fourfold.

By then, the ITF was fighting massive job losses caused by
containerisation in ports and mechanisation on the railways,
as well as running its campaign against shipowners using
"flags of convenience," which is still active today. The ITF
owned a ship, the MV Global Mariner, which sailed the
world drumming up support for the campaign, until in sank

in a collision in 2000.

STRUCTURE

Congress meets every four years, and elects a President and five Vice-Presidents representing global regions. Congress also elects a General Secratary who heads up the ITF's full-time staff, and an Executive Board of 40, which meets twice a year.

Any democratic union with members in the transport sector can affiliate to the ITF. As well as regional organisations, the ITF has a Women Transport Workers Committee and a Young Transport Workers Committee, and holds conferences for women and young members whenever Congress meets.

CAMPAIGNING

At the heart of ITF campaigning is the belief that strategic connections between unions representing transport workers and other types of workers is key to influencing the supply chain and movement of goods.

The ITF's longest-running campaign is its "Flags of Convenience" campaign, established in 1948. This came about due to the particular nature of the shipping industry, where owners can register ships in countries with poor labour laws, in order to get out of having to provide decent working conditions to their crew. This can make it impossible for national unions to take up the cause of these workers. The ITF therefore has an almost unique role among the GUFs as a direct negotiator on behalf of workers on FOC ships. The ITF issues certificates to those ships that sign up to its collective agreement. Currently it covers about a quarter of FOC ships, protecting 120,000 seafarers. A global network of 130 "ITF inspectors," full-time and part-time union officials, monitors conditions aboard FOC ships to ensure compliance with the agreement.

The ITF is concerned with the practice of shipping companies abandoning crew in foreign ports. Said El Hairech, a leader of the Moroccan dockers' union, campaigned against such an incident after the bankrupting of the Comarit-Comanav ferry company left crew members stranded in Spain. Said was jailed, and the ITF spearheaded an international campaign which secured his release. The ITF has put Said forward for the Febe Elisabeth Velasquez international trade union rights award.

Also in the maritime sector, the Federation's high-profile Global Network Terminals (GNT) Campaign targets multinational global terminal operators - APMT, DPW, HPH and PSA – who control up to 50% of the worlds ports and terminals. This campaign sees ITF unions leading the fight for acceptable standards for men and women working in ports and docks around the world – one of the most hazardous working environments there is.

Aviation is obviously another international industry with an international workforce. The ITF has brought together British and Spanish unions in the long-running restructuring dispute at Iberia, which is a sister company of British Airways. When Willie Walsh, the chief executive of the parent company International Airlines Group, stepped in to scupper negotiations with Iberia management, this international pressure forced him to back off.

In 1997, the ITF's road transport section undertook its first annual day of action on road safety. In 1999, affiliates brought out 200,000 workers on to the streets in Asia and Latin America, protesting against drivers' fatigue and long working hours. This has mushroomed into a week of action, and since 2008 rail unions have been involved as well. In October 2012 the week of action was called around the slogan "Transport workers fighting back! Organising globally!" Actions included go-slow lorry convoys in West Africa and Europe. In Nepal a 5km long taxi rally was organised in Kathmandu. The week of action also ties into the ongoing campaigns, for example to free persecuted members of the Tehran Bus Workers' Union in Iran.

Right now, one of the ITF's most important and active campaigns is against DHL, after the company's Turkish arm sacked workers who were organising a union in June 2012. The ITF unions worldwide along the supply chain have participated in days of action to condemn DHL's behaviour and support their comrades in Turkey. The campaign to organise and strengthen unions throughout the company, Respect at DHL, has built a sizeable online presence, and included a very visible protest at London Fashion Week, where DHL was the official logistics provider.

THE INTERNATIONAL UNION OF FOOD, AGRICULTURAL, HOTEL, RESTAURANT, CATERING, TOBACCO AND ALLIED WORKERS' ASSOCIATIONS

WWW.IUF.ORG

The global union for workers in agriculture, and the food production, catering, hotel, and tobacco industries.

*IUF represents **12 million** workers in **390** unions across **120** countries.*

PRESIDENT
Hans-Olof Nilsson

GENERAL SECRETARY
Ron Oswald

Rampe du Pont-Rouge, 8
CH-1213, Petit-Lancy
Switzerland

Phone: + 41 22 793 22 33
Fax: + 41 22 793 22 38
Email: iuf@iuf.org

HISTORY

The International Union of Food, Agricultural, Hotel, Restaurant, Catering, Tobacco and Allied Workers' Associations, or IUF for short, was founded in 1920 as a merger between international unions of bakers, brewers, and meat industry workers, all which had been in existence before the First World War.

The foundation of the IUF was a reaction to changes in the food and drink industry, which saw production increasingly fall under the control of huge, monopolistic conglomerates. The commitment the IUF still holds to organise workers along all stages of the food production chain therefore dates right back to its foundation.

The IUF began dealing with transnational companies as far back as 1963, when it brought together British and Pakistani tobacco workers to negotiate with British American Tobacco. In the early 1970s, the IUF began to bring together Nestle workers around the world. When Peruvian milk workers occupied the Chiclayo plant in 1973, the IUF launched an international campaign, which led to the New Zealand milk workers threatening to shut down their factory. Nestle caved and recognised the Peruvian union. By the 1990s, in the context of an ever more comprehensive process of globalisation, the IUF was strong enough to sign its first international agreements with multinationals Accor and Danone.

Post-war mergers strengthened the IUF, bringing in the international unions of tobacco workers (1958), and hotel, restaurant, and bar workers (1961). Geographically, the IUF spread beyond Europe, gaining affiliates in the Americas in the 1950s, and then in Africa and Asia, where a regional office was founded in Manila in the 1960s. Despite a rocky relationship with the AFL-CIO over operations in Latin America, the IUF managed to consolidate its regional organisations. A further merger with the Plantation Workers' International in 1994 ensured that the majority of IUF affiliates were now based in the global south.

STRUCTURE

Congress meets every five years, electing an executive committee that meets annually and has limited decision-making powers between congresses. The elected General Secretary heads up the full time staff in Geneva.

The IUF is organised into global regions and also has industrial groups for the food and drink industry, catering and tourism, agriculture, and tobacco industry.

CAMPAIGNING

The IUF's industrial position means that its affiliates are often organising in some of the biggest and most well-known multinational companies in the world, such as Kraft, Nestle, Unilever, Coca-Cola, and Hilton.

In the hotel industry, IUF affiliates are often organising, and campaigning for the rights of, casual workers. In the last year alone, the union has supported and publicised campaigns in hotels from Mumbai to Washington, DC, to Hilton in the Maldives.

At the last IUF Congress in 2012, the union launched its "We are the 53!" campaign, supporting sacked Nescafe workers in Panjang, Indonesia. The workers had been sacked after a long struggle for union recognition in their factory. The campaign resulted in a big win for the workers following an impressive display of solidarity by IUF-affiliated unions, including unions representing Nestle workers around the world.

The IUF frequently runs online campaigns for its affiliates, which allow supporters to easily send off messages of protest. Recently there have been campaigns against casualisation at Coca-Cola in the Philippines, and for the reinstatement of union leaders at Kraft sites in Egypt and Tunisia.

Here Jennie Formby, National Officer for the Food, Drink, and Tobacco section of Unite the Union in the UK, gives an insight into how her union works together with the IUF.

Can you give us a specific example where being a member of a global union federation has helped your union in a dispute with an employer or government?

During the takeover of Cadbury by Kraft, the IUF provided invaluable intelligence about the behaviour of Kraft globally that helped us to campaign, both with shareholders and with the UK Government. That campaign, whilst not able to prevent the takeover (which was dominated by short term hedge funds) led to the establishment of a Government Select Committee that not only questioned senior Executives in Kraft but which has kept a watching brief on developments since then. More importantly, it directly led to changes in the UK takeover law to ensure greater transparency and involvement of workers in takeovers; far from perfect but much better than previously

The subsequent national dispute over pensions in the UK led to strike action across all sites, and ultimately resulted in a settlement that was better than we could ever have hoped for. IUF helped in two ways; firstly by ensuring we had global solidarity - very much supported by Labour-Start! - which was very important in building the confidence of our members to keep fighting back, but very importantly, in working behind the scenes to persuade senior management to get round the table and talk to us, something that they had been strenuously resisting.

On a small scale, when we had a dispute at one of the Coke

sites in London, the IUF both raised issues with global management and also ensured our stewards on site got solidarity from all over the world that frankly blew them away and not only increased their confidence in fighting back, but made them feel they had a responsibility to keep fighting so as not to let down their comrades in other countries.

These are just three examples, I could give many others.

Has your union supported campaigns by your global union federation in other countries?

Unite always supports IUF campaigns and tries to take actions, however limited, to make sure we raise the visibility of those campaigns.

Our members strongly supported the 'CasualTea' campaign in a number of ways. We wrote letters both from our General Secretary but also from senior stewards across all sites to senior management, and raised the issues at national and European meetings to keep it on the agenda and to express our serious concerns about the way in which management were behaving. Members across the whole of our sector and in fact more widely in Unite supported the electronic campaign, and the postcard campaign.

We have supported other campaigns in the same way as above, for Nespresso and the "53" campaign, Unilever FNV workers in the Netherlands, and Kraft workers in Egypt where we are also now looking at twinning between our Bournville site and the Egyptian site. Others have included the "Hey Coke, Respect Workers' rights" campaign in the

Philippines, and the current "Screamdelez" campaign against the treatment of workers by Mondelez in Tunisia and Egypt.

Do you feel that the average member of your union is aware of your membership in a global union federation?

We do all we can to raise awareness of our members of the role of the GUF; I think there is pretty good awareness on the part of our shop stewards in general, particularly because we try to involve the IUF in training programmes for senior stewards, and there is also good awareness on the part of members where we have had campaigns but we're always looking for ways to build that awareness amongst shop floor members.

Other than campaigns, in what ways has your union benefited from membership in the international labour movement?

The IUF is extremely supportive in our education programmes and have participated in several national courses that we have run on transnational issues. They are also very supportive in terms of research and other background information that we need in fighting back and organising in specific companies. For example, [IUF Director of International Campaigns] Peter Rossman has given us great financial information that has helped us to highlight key issues when writing to management in respect of the planned takeover of Heinz, but we are also looking at building greater cooperation and networking following the takeover.

PUBLIC SERVICES
INTERNATIONAL

WWW.WORLD-PSI.ORG

*The global union for workers in the
public sector, including central and
local government, utilities, healthcare,
and social services.*

*PSI represents **20 million** workers in
650 unions across **148** countries.*

PRESIDENT
Dave Prentis

GENERAL SECRETARY
Rosa Pavanelli

45 avenue Voltaire
BP 9
01211 Ferney-Voltaire Cedex
France

Tel: +33(0)450406464
Fax: +33(0)450407320
Email: psi@world-psi.org

History

Public sector unions developed in Europe around the turn of the 20th century, as local governments, often influenced by social democrats, began to take over the running of services like water, gas, and electricity.

The first international meeting of these unions took place in Stuttgart in 1907, hot on the heels of the International Socialist Congress. Further meetings followed in Copenhagen in 1910, and Zurich in 1913. The Zurich meeting drew up a common list of demands, including the eight hour day, collective bargaining, and paid holidays. The secretariat maintained a skeletal existence during the First World War, and properly re-established itself in 1919. By the end of the postwar boom, in 1921, the PSI boasted nearly half a million members.

During the Depression, as well as fighting for the conditions of public sector workers, the PSI advocated a dramatic expansion of the public sector itself, calling for mines, heavy industry, and banks to be nationalised. In Scandinavia, the public sector unions managed to win laws dramatically improving job security and pensions.

But the rise of fascism elsewhere in Europe took its toll, as unions were banned or incorporated into state organisations. The PSI secretariat had to leave Berlin after Hitler came to power, moving to Paris where, initially, its operations were run out of a private flat with typewriters on loan from other unions. The PSI was forced to suspend its activities when the Nazis captured Paris in 1940, but managed to regroup, along with other international trade secretariats, in London.

Post-war conditions faced by PSI affiliates were contradictory. The welfare state led to a huge expansion of the public sector across industrialised countries. However, the Cold War mentality of the 1950s led to bans on strikes for municipal workers in Japan and many US states, and for civil servants in many countries.

PSI affiliates in some countries were slow to catch on to the need to link with workers' organisations in former colonies. General Secretary Maarten Bolle, who had made a great effort to meet with unions across Asia, resigned in protest when the British National Union of General and Municipal Employees refused to pay into the PSI solidarity fund.

The PSI held its first regional conferences for Africa and Asia in 1965, responding to pressure from unions wanting more local decision-making structures. Over the 1970s, these developed into Regional Advisory Committees which attracted many more affiliates from the global south. In the 1980s the PSI was able to step up its international solidarity work, helping imprisoned trade unionists in countries such as Chile and Turkey. In 1989 a campaign by the PSI and Amnesty International won the acquittal of five healthworkers in South Africa who had been accused of treason by the apartheid government for their union activities.

The neo-liberal offensive which began in the 1970s threatened all unions, but particularly PSI affiliates because of the assault on the public sector. In Chile under the dictatorship, for example, 25% was cut from all public spending (except the military). From the 1980s, public sector unions were fighting for their very existence. Margaret Thatcher banned unions from organising at GCHQ (a branch of the intelligence services) in Britain, for example, while health workers unions around the world suffered from massive spending cuts as services were privatised.

The PSI responded by engaging in an ideological battle, trying to rehabilitate the public sector in the eyes of a general public bombarded with free market propaganda. As well as educating its own members to take on the arguments of neo-liberalism, the PSI was able to expand its training programmes into eastern Europe with the collapse of the Berlin Wall. In doing so, the PSI was able to dampen some of the understandable enthusiasm for free market policies that had developed among many workers in the former Stalinist states.

STRUCTURE

Congress, the top decision-making body of PSI, meets every five years, and is made up of delegates from affiliated unions. Delegates elect a President and General Secretary by simple majority vote.

Between Congresses, PSI is run by an Executive Board, made up of representatives from each region, who are nominated by their regional executives and approved by Congress. There are seats on the Executive Board for one young worker from each region, and larger affiliates with over 500,000 members are entitled to a seat.

Extraordinary Congresses can be called by the Executive Board, or by affiliates representing one-third of the PSI's membership.

At its 29th World Congress in Durban in November 2012, PSI elected its first woman general secretary, Rosa Pavanelli.

CAMPAIGNING

The PSI and its affiliates have to confront the ongoing privatisation of vital services, which, as well as being a hot political issue, brings with it many workplace problems. Outsourced workers are often on worse contracts, with precarious hours and fewer employment benefits.

In 2010, the PSI brought together its Turkish affiliates to agree a joint strategy for tackling precarious employment. The campaign led to collective bargaining agreements being signed, some 6,000 temp workers having their status changed back to permanent, and over 20,000 new recruits for the unions.

In the last couple of years, the PSI has helped its affiliates in South America establish functioning, self-run youth committees. The project has trained young workers in collective bargaining techniques in order to equip them to take on the blight of precarious work, and formed an alliance between young workers and the University Students Confederation.

As well as this campaigning, the independent Public Services International Research Unit, based at the University of Greenwich in London, works with PSI to investigate privatisation and restructuring in public services around the world. The PSIRU holds databases on the activities of multinational companies who are profiting from privatisation, making it a valuable resource for trade unionists facing up to the problems of globalisation.

PSI was a key player in the global movement to achieve the Human Right to Clean Water and Sanitation, formally recognised by the United Nations in 2010.

PSI has also been active in the global movement for a financial transactions tax, also known as the Robin Hood Tax, working with unions and allies to organise major lobbying events in connection with the G20 in 2011, G8 and Rio+20 in 2012, and the World Social Forum in Tunisia, World Bank/IMF, and Sustainable Development Goals meetings in 2013. PSI is currently working with its European branch, EPSU, and affiliates in other regions to advance the international tax justice movement.

General Secretary Rosa Pavanelli gave a speech at the UN in March 2013 on the issue of public service workers' rights and the need for strong public services in order to effectively plan for and respond to major disasters including earthquakes and hurricanes. PSI also launched an "End violence against women" campaign on 8 March 2013.

**UNION NETWORK
INTERNATIONAL
GLOBAL UNION**

WWW.UNIGLOBALUNION.ORG

*The global union for service sector workers,
including cleaning and security, commerce,
finance, gaming, graphical and packaging,
hair and beauty, the information
communication technology and services
industry (ICTS), media, post and logistics
and private care.*

PRESIDENT
Joe de Bruyn

GENERAL SECRETARY
Phillip Jennings

8-10 Avenue Reverdil
CH-1260 NYON
Switzerland

Tel: +41 22 365 21 00
Fax: + 41 22 365 21 21
Email:
contact@uniglobalunion.org

HISTORY

UNI Global Union was founded on 1st January 2000, as a merger of no fewer than four international labour organisations: The Communications International, the International Graphical Federation, the Media and Entertainment International, and FIET (the white collar and global services union).

STRUCTURE

Congress takes place every four years, accompanied by a World Women's Conference. The last Congress was held in Nagasaki, Japan, in 2010. The next one will be in Cape Town in 2014.

Regional offices are located in Abidjan, Brussels, Johannesburg, Montevideo, Singapore, and Tokyo.

CAMPAIGNING

In 2010 UNI adopted its "Breaking Through" strategy, which focuses on the growth of unions in UNI sectors in order to secure economic justice for working people. As part of this strategy, all of UNI sectors aim to build unions and win organising rights, and they implement campaigns for that purpose with affiliates within the sectors. UNI's Strategic Campaigns, Organising, Research, and Education department (UNI SCORE) supports this work. Current campaigns to win organising rights include DHL, Walmart, Prosegur and Deutsche Telekom. UNI actively supports the organising campaigns of its affiliates in about 50 countries.

As part of its goal to promote organising, UNI gives recognition to its affiliates who are fighting to grow their unions. Recent "Breaking Through" award winners have included: the Turkish Tez-Koop-Is union, which has successfully won recognition after recruiting nearly 60% of Tesco employees in the country; the Argentinian union FAECYS, which recruited over 1,000 members in a call centre organising drive which led to negotiating rights with two multinational companies; and Dutch union FNV Bondgenoten which ran a nine week campaign of industrial action, winning a 3.5% pay rise for cleaners.

As of April 2013, UNI had signed 48 Global Framework Agreements with multinationals, including security giants G4S and Securitas, fashion chain H&M, cleaning contractor ISS, and the Banco de Brasil.

UNI is co-ordinating a global campaign to win worker and union rights at the world's biggest retailer, Walmart. UNI has won oversight and raised the issue of worker protection for Walmart workers in South Africa. In India, UNI has joined with local NGOs and other allies to campaign against allowing Walmart to enter the country without conditions to protect local communities and workers, bringing light to Walmart's poor global track record on labour rights. The UNI

Walmart Global Union Alliance was launched in Los Angeles in October 2012 and gave backing to the first strike in the company's 50 year history.

The theme of the Cape Town 2014 Congress will be "Including You" which encompasses the fight for union growth; the promotion of a new, fairer sustainable global economy; and the world of work where quality jobs, collective bargaining and social protection will be the keys to success in an increasingly volatile global labour market.

Prakash Baral, President of Ncell Employees Trade Union (NETU - Nepal), tells us how his union benefits from being part of UNI.

Can you give us a specific example where being a member of a global union federation has helped your union in a dispute with an employer or government?

We have had several situations of this kind where we have been able to resolve the dispute with the help of UNI Global Union and specifically through its regional body UNI APRO.

Two particular situations were very critical. Firstly, during the establishment of the union, UNI played an important role in helping us to encourage workers to be united and in getting management to accept the union.

Secondly, during our first CBA negotiations in 2009, strike action was avoided due to the support of UNI / UNI APRO who helped discussions move more positively. We benefited from their coaching and international experience and were able to think more broadly. During these negotiations we also benefited from having Swedish and Finnish trade union representatives with us, thanks to UNI/UNI APRO.

Has your union supported campaigns by your global union federation in other countries?

Not directly but our success stories are told and shared in other countries like Moldova and Cambodia. UNI Global Union has brought us together with a union in Moldova and we are encouraging our Cambodian brothers working in Smart Mobile to get organised; with the support of UNI APRO this work has been strongly coordinated and last year, 2012, they won union recognition. We are enthusiastically and actively supporting UNI's campaign on union recognition and organising workers in Teliasonera operations in other countries too.

Do you feel that the average member of your union is aware of your membership in a global union federation?

Yes, they are aware of our membership with UNI Global Union. We communicate with them via all-staff mail about different kinds of activities with UNI. All the members are proud of being with UNI Global Union.

Other than campaigns, in what ways has your union benefited from membership in the international labour movement?

When dealing with management it is very positive for us being part of the international labour movement. We have been getting support in different ways, creating a positive environment. Through UNI/UNI APRO we have been hosting joint meetings with Finnish and Swedish unions; as they are unions from the company headquarters, this has encouraged us very much. UNI/UNI APRO also provides various training courses to assist us in developing our skills on negotiation and CBA. Much of the support is for workers' solidarity which really adds strength to our workforce.

OTHER INTERNATIONAL BODIES

INTERNATIONAL TRADE UNION CONFEDERATION

ITUC CSI IGB

WWW.ITUC-CSI.ORG

PRESIDENT

Michael Sommer

GENERAL SECRETARY

Sharan Burrow

Boulevard du Roi Albert II, 5,
Bte 1
1210 Brussels
Belgium

Tel: +32 (0)2 224 0211
Fax: +32 (0)2 201 5815
Email: info@ituc-csi.org

HISTORY

The ITUC was founded at a Congress in Vienna in 2006 which brought together the International Confederation of Free Trade Unions (ICFTU) and the smaller World Confederation of Labour (WCL), as well as unions previously without an international affiliation.

Attempts to create an international trade union organisation date back to before the First World War, when unions from European countries came together to set up an International Secretariat. Like many labour organsiations, this effectively ceased to function after 1914. After the war, it was refounded as the social democratic International Federation of Trade Unions (IFTU).

The IFTU reached an affiliated membership of 24 million – mostly European – workers between the wars, before fascist regimes started to persecute and destroy unions, and the Second World War prevented the organisation from functioning properly, just like its predecessor.

In 1945, the World Federation of Trade Unions (WFTU) was formed. It aspired to bring trade unions in the Communist and non-Communist worlds together in a single organisation, somewhat mirroring developments at the United Nations.

However, as the iron curtain descended and the Cold War began to heat up, ideological differences could not be ignored. Free unions found it impossible to work with organisations that were essentially organs of state control in countries like the USSR. In particular, Communist-led unions were in opposition to the Marshall Plan, seeing it as primarily an attempt by the USA to gain influence in post-war Europe.

This led most union centres in the West to leave the WFTU in 1949, and set up the ICFTU. They included the British TUC, the Italian CISL, and both major American union federations, the AFL and the CIO. A minority, like the French CGT, stayed in the WFTU.

The ICFTU was able to go beyond the European limits of its predecessor fairly quickly, attracting two union centres from India, and a number of Brazilian unions. During the Cold War, it upheld the ideas of free trade unionism against dictatorships of all types, providing assistance both to workers in Eastern Europe, and the Spanish UGT carrying out underground activity in fascist Spain.

After the end of the Cold War, unions from or closely aligned with the Communist tradition joined the ITUC, such as the French CGT (1995). The South African union centre COSATU also affiliated, although debates currently rage in the organisation about international affiliation, and some member unions have joined the WFTU.

STRUCTURE

Since its founding Congress in 2006, the ITUC has held a second Congress in Vancouver in 2010. The next one will take place in Berlin in 2014. Congress elects a General Council of 78 members. Of these, 70 are elected on a regional basis, six are nominated by the Womens Committee, and two are nominated by the Youth Committee.

The General Council elected an Executive Board of up to 25 members, which deals with urgent matters between the annual meetings of the Council.

The ITUC works with the global union federations in the Council of Global Unions, through which various statements of international union policy are published and presented to bodies like the International Monetary Fund.

There are currently four regional organisations, for Europe, the Americas, Asia-Pacific, and Africa. The President and the General Secretary, elected by Congress, cannot come from the same region.

The ITUC has five departments, covering Campaigns, Equality, Finance, Policy, and Human and Trade Union Rights.

CAMPAIGNING

The ITUC has been involved in the Play Fair campaign, within which it has worked with the BWI and IndustriALL, to highlight the conditions of workers at and in the lead up to high profile sporting events like the Olympics.

Last year the ITUC launched its 12 by 12 campaign, pushing for governments to ratify ILO Convention 189 on domestic work. Coming in to force in September 2013, the convention has currently been ratified by Uruguay, Italy, and the Philippines thanks to union pressure.

Since 2007, October 7th has been marked by the ITUC as the World Day for Decent Work. In 2012 the actions ranged from Indonesia to Burma, Bulgaria to Senegal, and focused on the burning problem of youth unemployment.

Each year, the ITUC produces its survey of labour violations around the world. This country-by-country guide is an invaluable resource for activists and NGOs monitoring the repression of trade unionists. In each country for which information is available, the survey describes the conditions trade unionists are working in, and documents arrests, summary killings by the state and other forces, and changes in labour law that restrict union activity.

Recently, the ITUC has launched the online publication *Equal Times*, in English, French, and Spanish. *Equal Times* carries news and analysis of unions around the world, as well as promoting campaigns.

TRADE UNION ADVISORY COMMITTEE TO THE OECD

WWW.TUAC.ORG

PRESIDENT
Richard Trumka

GENERAL SECRETARY
John Evans

15 rue Lapérouse - 75016
Paris
France

Tel : +33 (0) 1 55 37 37 37
Fax : +33 (0) 1 47 54 98 28
E-mail: tuac@tuac.org

History

TUAC was founded in 1948, as the trade union advisory committee during the Marshall Plan. With the founding of the Organisation for Economic Co-Operation and Development in 1961, TUAC reprised its role as the voice presenting the views of unions to the organisation.

Structure

The TUAC secretariat consists of five policy staff and three administrative staff. The policy staff are each responsible for a number of areas of work. These are as varied as climate change, pension funds, migration, employment, and education.

TUAC holds a plenary session twice a year, to which all affiliates are invited. These sessions set the policy, priorities, and budget of TUAC, as well as electing an Administrative Committee made up of representatives from affiliates, the President, Vice-presidents and General Secretary.

Campaigning

TUAC meets with the various committees and bodies of the

OECD, as well as its member governments, to present the views and policies of the international labour movement. It is responsible, working alongside the ITUC, for co-ordinating the input of the unions into international summits like the G8 and G20. The OECD also consults with TUAC at the relevant meetings of ministers from its member nations (for example, employment ministers).

TUAC's work has led to the improvement of OECD guidelines for multinationals, making sure that clauses have covered child labour and forced labour. TUAC promotes these guidelines to trade unionists around the world, and helps to monitor their implementation.

Together with the ITUC and PSI, TUAC has set up an anti-corruption network called UNICORN, which monitors corruption and bribery, and campaigns for legal protection for whistleblowers who expose such practices.

THE COUNCIL OF GLOBAL UNIONS

The Council of Global Unions, established in 2007, brings together the GUFs, the ITUC, and TUAC. It is not an organisation, but a tool to encourage co-operation between the organisations of the international labour movement. To that end, the CGU has established working groups on migration, public services, and a special working group on Burma/Myanmar. Its website also links to details of every global framework agreement won by all the GUFs.

Many statements developed by the ITUC and TUAC for the consideration of bodies like the G20 and the International Monetary Fund are issued under the name of "Global Unions" to underline this unity.

The Council is based in Brussels. It is co-ordinated by Jim Baker, its President is the ITUC's Sharan Burrow, and its Chair is Ambet Yuson.

Email: jim.baker@global-unions.org

WORKING WITH THE INTERNATIONAL LABOUR MOVEMENT

THE BRITISH TUC'S INTERNATIONAL WORK

Owen Tudor, Head of European and International Relations Department, TUC

The TUC belongs to three international trade union organisations – the European Trade Union Confederation (ETUC), ITUC and TUAC – and we play a leading role in all three, as well as in the Workers Group at the International Labour Organisation and in lots of informal international groupings.

Our formal involvement means that we are represented on a lot of committees and mailing lists, but we try to make sure our contribution is deeper than the formalities suggest (see box).

Our links with unions in Europe are, of course, mostly aimed at influencing the European Union, which sets the legal and increasingly economic framework for the UK. The ETUC gives us access to – and a collective voice in – decisions about Directives covering workplace rights, multilateral and bilateral trade negotiations, equality laws and so on.

And we also bargain with employers at European level over issues like agency work, part-time workers' rights, working from home and maternity arrangements. The 'social dialogue' as it is called has produced agreements that the EU has turned into legal rights, although in recent years the lack of political pressure on employers has meant most social dialogue agreements have set frameworks and encouraged best practice.

The TUC has been keen also to encourage unions across Europe to use the ETUC to develop campaigns against austerity and inequality, as well as for workers' rights and economic democracy. So far, campaigns against specific legislation – such as the Services Directive – have been more successful than attempts to change the political weather.

Globally, we use the international trade union movement as an arena where we can work more closely with sister trade unions on specific issues such as delivering solidarity to unions in Colombia (and applying lessons learnt by US unions about their country's free trade deal with Colombia to the EU's negotiations on a similar deal).

Or on global developments like climate change, where TUC official Philip Pearson was for several years the chair of the ITUC environment network which developed policy and co-ordinated action over the UN climate change negotiations, making sure that 'just transition' was included in the texts governments were working on.

The campaign for a Robin Hood Tax is a major issue for UK unions concerned about the need to rebalance the economy and raise revenue to reduce cuts in public services. But we have used the European trade union movement to secure the support of 11 EU member states for a Robin Hood Tax, and worked with colleagues in the Washington DC office of the ITUC to influence the International Monetary Fund's response to the idea (which moved from hostile, to neutral and beyond as a direct result of evidence-based union lobbying!)

We're also involved in lots of smaller groupings drawn from the international movement and facilitated by the ITUC, which we use to co-ordinate international trade union solidarity for workers in countries like Fiji, Iran, and Swaziland.

Work on Fiji, for instance, has involved a small group of national trade union centres and relevant Global Union Federations who are willing to do the heavy lifting, teleconferencing to plan actions which are then rolled out to be taken by a much larger group, putting pressure on the regime through the ILO, embassy protests, and corporate leveraging strategies.

We've also used this mechanism to carry out direct lobbying of the Australian, New Zealand, UK and US Foreign Ministers (who operate an informal Fiji 'quartet') by the trade union movements in those four countries.

Fiji and Swaziland, of course, are also members of the Commonwealth, and the ITUC convenes a Commonwealth Trade Union Group (CTUG) which meets annually at the ILO, and is increasingly involved in effective solidarity work as well as lobbying the Commonwealth itself, including through the biennial Commonwealth Heads of Government Meeting where a CTUG delegation engages with civil society and Foreign Ministers.

The TUC is working with newly united Swazi trade union

centre TUCOSWA to campaign for the last feudal dictatorship in Africa to be suspended for not meeting Commonwealth standards of democracy and human rights.

Individual unions in the UK do of course have their own
international contacts – especially through the Global Union
Federations – so the TUC is only occasionally involved in
transnational labour disputes. But as corporations become
more globalised, we are increasingly using the international
union structures to form links which help unions lobby
companies in other countries, and advising unions on taking
cases under the OECD's code of practice for multinational
enterprises, such as over G4S and Unilever.

The G20 is another forum where unions have used international structures to maximise our lobbying influence. In the
days ahead of each G20 leaders' summit, a team of union
leaders from the G20 countries – including the UK – has met
with the host and several participants as well as the heads of
international institutions such as the IMF, World Trade Organisation and, of course, the ILO.

Known irreverently by global leaders as 'speed dating', this
co-ordinated last minute lobbying of leaders like Australia's
Julia Gillard, Brazil's Dilma Rousseff and, yes, even our own
Prime Minister David Cameron, is of course based on
months of preparatory work around a trade union submis-
sion developed through TUAC. It is the envy of NGOs who
are often outside the G20, protesting but not being heard by
world leaders who can't avoid listening to the arguments of
the world's largest people's movement.

The TUC's role in global trade unionism is well-respected by trade unionists and others around the world, and never has that been better reflected than by the election last year of Guy Ryder – who started his career at the TUC as an international officer – as the first ever worker representative to become Director-General of the ILO.

The TUC and the international unions

The TUC affiliates to the European Trade Union Confederation (ETUC) representing 60 million workers; the International Trade Union Confederation (ITUC), representing 175 million workers worldwide, as well as their jointly-run Pan-European Regional Council; and the Trade Union Advisory Committee to the OECD (TUAC).

Our General Secretary, Frances O'Grady, is a member of the ETUC Executive Committee and Steering Committee; the ITUC General Council and Executive Bureau; and the Management Committee of TUAC. Sally Hunt, the TUC General Council spokesperson on international relations and General Secretary of lecturers' union UCU, sits on both the ETUC Executive Committee (along with Billy Hayes – General Council Europe spokesperson and CWU General Secretary – and Dave Prentis, General Secretary of Unison) and the ITUC General Council. Diana Holland, from Unite, is the chair of the ITUC Women's Committee and therefore sits on the General Council and Executive Bureau, and Gloria Mills from Unison is on the Bureau of the ETUC Women's Committee and also sits on the Executive. At the ILO, Sam Gurney from the TUC is a member of the Governing Body as one of 14 Workers Group representatives. The TUC also has a member – usually the relevant TUC staff member – on each of the ETUC working groups and committees covering issues like trade, workers' rights, economic policy and so on.

THE GLOBAL LABOUR INSTITUTE

Dave Spooner, GLI UK

The Global Labour Institute (GLI Network Ltd) is an international network of organisations aiming to promote international solidarity among trade union organisations and affiliated groups in order to achieve a democratic and sustainable world society.

In particular, the network develops and encourages education, capacity-building and research on international labour movement development, gender policy and organising strategies. The GLI Network works closely with a range of global union federations, national trade unions, workers' associations, development agencies, research institutions and workers' education organisations, and is guided by its principles of democratic socialism.

The first Global Labour Institute was established in Geneva in 1997 and is chaired by Dan Gallin, a former General Secretary of the International Union of Foodworkers (IUF). Global Labour Institutes were also established at Cornell University, New York, and in Manchester UK, forming the GLI Network, subsequently joined by the Praxis Center in Moscow, and planned further GLIs in Bulgaria and Greece.

Whilst acting independently, the GLIs are united in their shared analysis of the global challenges facing the labour movement. This analysis states that the globalisation of the world economy has led to: an enormous increase of transnational corporate power acting in consensus with conservative governments, ubiquitous neo-liberalism, exploitation and oppression, the denigration of labour and human rights, entrenched gender inequality, the destruction of the environment and the rise of various forms of fascism and war.

The GLIs are further united in their commitment to supporting the international trade union movement to tilt the global balance of power away from conservative governments and transnational corporate power towards a democratic and sustainable world society. They aim to facilitate this through rescuing labour history and strengthening the identity of the labour movement, encouraging a new programme and political vision for the movement in cooperation with like-minded movements and organisations, inspiring global trade union organisation, and facilitating networks of solidarity between trade unions and like-minded groups of civil society.

The GLIs conduct research and create publications in concert with their aims, run educational activities with national and international trade union partners, and establish meetings and facilitate networking among like-minded organisations to encourage a collective programme of action. In summer 2012 the GLI UK established the first International Summer School for the international trade union movement, achieving a key objective established at the founding of GLI Geneva. The summer school brought together unionists from across the world to debate what are, and what should be, the politics of the international trade union movement, and encouraged a renewed political vision.

The 2013 International Summer School is set to take place in July 2013 at Northern College, UK, with other similar events planned in Athens and Manila.

GLI Contacts:

Geneva:	www.global-labour.org
New York:	www.ilr.cornell.edu/globallaborinstitute
Manchester:	www.global-labour.net
Moscow:	www.praxiscenter.ru/about_us/english

AMNESTY INTERNATIONAL'S ROLE

Shane Enright, Global Trade Union Adviser, Amnesty International

Amnesty International celebrated its fiftieth anniversary a couple of years ago. One of the first 'prisoners of conscience' we campaigned for back in 1961 was Toni Ambatielos, a maritime trade union leader jailed in Greece. Within two years he was out of jail.

Insisting on workers' rights has been part of Amnesty International's lifeblood from the start. Whether defending trade unionists under Apartheid, in Communist Poland, in Pinochet's Chile, or today in Colombia, Fiji, Zimbabwe, Turkey, the Philippines, and elsewhere, Amnesty has been steadfast when workers' rights are repressed.

But we have not always been collaborative. Amnesty International used to believe that its impartiality – our powerful asset of independent verifiable research – meant we had to stay aloof from the organisations and movements whose civil and political, social and economic, rights we defended.

That has all changed within the past decade. Our vision these days is one of active participation by rights holders; of strategic partnerships and coalitions, and comes with a strong measure of humility; trade unions were defending workers' rights long before we appeared on the scene and those who know best are the human rights defenders in the frontline of our struggles – the migrants organising in Singapore, Seoul and Doha; the trade unionists under fire in Belarus, Bahrain and Bangladesh.

The key to effective collaboration is to understand each other's strengths and perspectives; knowing the boundaries of what we can or cannot do together. The global unions, for instance, have a far larger membership than Amnesty, and a presence in countries of strategic influence where Amnesty is absent, but not all of these members or unions see beyond the workplace.

On the other hand, Amnesty's 3-million supporters are largely can-do hands-on activists, experienced, persistent and tenacious. The global unions are coordinating bodies, which are sometimes constrained by the common denominator, or by competing politics, of their affiliates. Individual unions, on the other hand, are entirely autonomous.

In contrast, Amnesty International is a much more centralised organisation with globally-set priorities, country strategies and approved casework. Arguably that makes us more efficient and disciplined, but it can make us cumbersome.

What matters to us all is human rights impact. When we are able to align our casework, to react together to country crises, or to share expertise and intelligence on issues of mutual concern, such as justice for "comfort women" or indigenous people's rights, that means a wiser use of resources, better distribution for appeals, and improved outcomes.

Our collaboration with the IUF saw protests in the past from Mozambique, Russia and Brazil to defend agricultural workers from violent evictions in Zimbabwe and to support their exiled union leader Gertrude Hambira.

Our joint appeal with the ITF and LabourStart when jailed Iranian bus leader Mansour Ossanloo was at risk of losing his eyesight saw him transferred from prison to hospital.

Su Su Nway is a young activist in Burma who stood up against forced labour and was jailed for peacefully advocating democratic change. Joint activism led by UK and global unions, backed by 40,000 solidarity and protest messages in Amnesty's "Write for Rights" campaign two years ago, resulted in her early release from a lengthy prison sentence.

Trade unionists understand well the interdependence of human rights. Sometimes our biggest challenge might not be labour rights abuses themselves but other fundamental human rights shortcomings. Amongst the most intractable and pernicious is the challenge of impunity; the absence of justice and accountability for acts of violence and threats against trade unionists and other community activists which is rife in Colombia, Guatemala, the Philippines and elsewhere. Judicial and security force corruption needs to be chipped away at through reinforcing fundamental civil rights, through strengthening international justice and accountability mechanisms and by addressing underlying systemic failures.

At the heart of our approach, and working alongside trade unions, is building and defending the capacity of human rights defenders on the ground.

Some of Amnesty's human rights agenda chimes with the wider social aspirations of trade unions. When we campaigned for safer schools for girls, we made common cause with Education International and teachers across continents.

Our up-coming priority campaign to promote women's sexual and reproductive rights must necessarily also include a call for more and better public health services, and better trained and rewarded health care workers.

Freedom of expression, assembly and association are also permanent concerns, and working with journalists and defending their unions is common ground for us all.
Knowing each other's limits is also critical.

Amnesty International does not and would not intervene in trade disputes or strikes unless fundamental rights are at stake. When the South Korean police dropped liquefied teargas on a factory being occupied by striking car workers, we said "enough is enough" but that doesn't mean we have any authority or competence to comment on the redundancies and employment issues at the heart of their struggle.

We are fortunate in Amnesty International that the UK Section has had a dynamic trade union network for over thirty years, and that we have hired expertise from a trade union background to help build and sustain our global relationships.

The technology of protest may have changed; telegrams were replaced by telexes, faxes were overtaken by emails, and now we have sms; Amnesty's *pocket protest* tool. But whatever our tools and our methods, the multiplying effect of collaboration and of making common cause will bear human rights dividends.

While our global relationships are strong, the greatest opportunity and impact will come from reinforcing local collaboration and cooperation. Amnesty Turkey has reached out to trade unionists who are seeking labour law reform; the result has been the biggest postcard appeal we've ever undertaken in Turkey; 20,000 protests presented to the government, and a trebling of Amnesty's activist base in that country.

In France, in Scandinavia, in Austria and elsewhere we have strong relationships on the ground, but we need to grow these, to leverage our global collaboration to make common cause within our communities. This represents the greatest opportunity as we defend workers' rights and human rights whether in Wisconsin or Fiji.

This year marks another anniversary – the fortieth year since the 'invention' of the Urgent Action as a citizen's tool to challenge repression and to protect individuals at risk. The first UA was sent worldwide on 19 March 1973, on behalf of Luiz Basilio Rossi, a Brazilian labour rights activist. He believed that Amnesty International's appeals were crucial:

"I knew that my case had become public, I knew they could no longer kill me. Then the pressure on me decreased and conditions improved."

He was released that same year.

An introduction to ICTUR

Daniel Blackburn, Director, ICTUR

Since its founding in 1987, the fundamental purpose of the International Centre for Trade Union Rights (ICTUR) has been to defend and improve trade union rights. These purposes are expressed in the organisation's Constitution in the following terms:

- to defend and extend the rights of trade unions and trade unionists throughout the world
- to collect information and increase awareness of trade union rights and their violations
- to carry out its activities in the spirit of the United Nations Charter, the Universal Declaration of Human Rights, the International Labour Organisation Conventions and appropriate international treaties.

In pursuing these objectives, ICTUR has won recognition on the global stage for its diligent work and for its legal and technical expertise. In 1993 ICTUR was granted accredited status with both the United Nations and the International Labour Organisation.

Our work involves:

- a human rights role to promote and defend trade union rights
- information sharing and advice
- providing legal, technical and research services
- projects to promote trade union rights.

Our key strengths are labour law, industrial relations, and human rights. Lawyers, unions, and human rights organisations participate. The international office serves a global hub on trade union rights. More than fifty national trade unions are affiliated to ICTUR. ICTUR's global membership also includes human rights organisations, research institutes and lawyers' associations. ICTUR bridges these realms of expertise and brings together unparalleled legal expertise on international trade union rights.

ICTUR is politically and organisationally independent and its activities are supervised through international structures, including: the Executive Committee, the senior lawyers and trade unionists who exercise management control over the organisation; the Administrative Council, which opens IC-TUR's work to public scrutiny and debate; and the Editorial Board, a forum for academic discussion.

One of our most well known activities is as a labour rights publisher. You may have seen our world map of trade union rights wall poster, free to access online, and which can now be found tacked to the walls in union offices across the globe. Or you may have encountered our journal *International Union Rights,* which is now in its 20th year of publication. IUR has earned its place as the leading independent forum for global union debate, and it now enjoys a readership across more than 100 countries worldwide.

Just over one year ago, in December 2011, striking oil workers in Kazakhstan were fired upon en masse by State forces, 12 were killed and dozens seriously injured. In August 2012 34 striking workers were shot dead and dozens more were seriously injured in the Marikana massacre in South Africa. In much of Europe labour rights were dismantled under direct pressure from the IMF/EU Troika, while in Greece repression of protests on the ground escalated in January 2013 when the police forced workers back to their jobs.

Added to this, workers faced an assault on the very foundation of their rights when, at the June 2012 Conference of the International Labour Organisation, employers denied the legal basis of the right to strike and walked out of a key committee, effectively shutting down one of the main structures of the ILO tasked with monitoring labour rights violations.

ICTUR has researched, reported upon, and responded to each of these cases.

Rights remain under grave threat in key countries such as Colombia and Turkey, where ICTUR has carried out long-running legal projects in support of trade union rights. But the increasingly hostile global situation means that ICTUR's work is currently urgently needed in numerous other countries and on diverse technical and legal questions.

When the Gibraltar section of the Unite trade union complained of complex layers of discrimination suffered by their Moroccan migrant members, ICTUR responded to the call and helped the union to analyse the legal situation.

If your union can affiliate to ICTUR, at local or national level, your support would make a real difference. We look forward to hearing from you, and we welcome the opportunity to cooperate with people and organisations worldwide.

Find out more at www.ictur.org

About LabourStart

This book has been published by LabourStart, the news and campaigning website of the international trade union movement.

We co-ordinate a network of hundreds of volunteer correspondents and translators, to post union news and campaigns from around the world. We regularly work with many of the organisations listed in this book.

To find out more, including how to donate to us or become a correspondent, visit www.labourstart.org.

You can read more about our campaigns in our previous book, *Campaigning Online and Winning,* available on Amazon, CreateSpace, and Kindle.

Made in the USA
Charleston, SC
29 April 2013